THIS COLOURING MAGAZINE BELONGS TO

____

COVER AND INTERIOR ILLUSTRATIONS BY
SIRREESE AND A. CLARKE
TEXT BY A. CLARKE.

MEET THE RENAISSANCE FEMALES

WWW.SIRREESE.COM

Milann

Angelees

PARISS

LONDONN

Milann

Angelees

Carlisle Bay

During the 17th and 18th century, Carlisle Bay Harbour was very important, as it received slaves from Africa. The Harbour became a trading place for precious local commodities, such as sugar and tobacco. Barbados became a major transshipment port of the eastern Caribbean.

Being formed completely of coral reefs and many fascinating shipwrecks, Carlisle Bay Area is one of the most picturesque areas in Barbados. It is home to four beaches, Pebbles Beach, Browne's Beach, Adventure Beach, Daiquiri Beach and a Marine Park. Carlisle Bay is a nice tranquil location just on the outskirts of Bridgetown with an abundance of marine life including rare species of sea horses, frog fish, bat fish, barracudas, octopus, reef squid, mackerel, moray eel and many more creatures. Clear waters excellent for snorkelling, underwater photography and Scuba diving.

Carlisle Bay Wrecks

The Eillion is a Scuba divers favourite shipwreck due to its easy access, a former 110 ft long drug vessel that was sunk in 1996 in 50ft water.

A different wreck that is a highlight for snorkellers is the Bajan Queen, it was Barbados' first tugboat named the "Pelican" in the 1960's. 10 years later the Pelican was converted into a party boat called "Bajan Queen". Years after living out its time as a party spot, the Bajan Queen was donated to the Coastal Zone Management Unit.

2002 it was cleaned up and sunk in 40ft of water in Carlisle Bay Marine Park.

Chattel House

As you travel around the island you will see many examples of the slave constructed Chattel Houses, a distinct form of architecture that is unique to Barbados, with vivid colours that show the West African influence. Former slaves were allowed to build a wooden house and rest it on a base of coral stone blocks on a piece of plantation land but because they did not own the land, the houses could not be built on a permanent foundation, in case it had to be moved. As a man's movable possessions were called his chattels, hence the name Chattel House. Even though the chattel house originated from humble origins, the chattel house evolved into a carefully planned structure. Ingenious solutions were required and produced to deal with notably high temperatures and heavy rains of the tropics. The angle of the steep gable roof deflects the wind. Demerara windows, the fretwork around the windows were placed there to provide shade and a filter against the rain. High ventilated gables and "tray" ceilings all came into use.

Parliament Buildings

Although Parliament was established in 1639, the Parliament buildings were not constructed until the end of the 19th century, two buildings, the East and West Wing. Built entirely of hand-cut and carved local coral limestone the West Wing is of neo-Gothic architectural style. It was finished in 1872 where the Barbados Museum of Parliament and the Barbados National Heroes Gallery are housed. Since 1884 a prominent feature attached to the west-wing is the clock tower with four clocks one on each side, which can be seen from different points around Bridgetown. Before 1884 the clock tower was attached to the east-wing, but due to poor soil conditions the clock tower was sinking. The tower was reconstructed at the west wing where it stands today.

The East Wing was completed in late 1873 and was built in British Victorian styled architecture. In November the Parliament Buildings are lit up in the colours of the national flag and in December green or red for Christmas.

National Heroes' Day

National Heroes Day is a public holiday in Barbados.

Barbados has been shaped by the vision, determination, commitment and achievements of some brave men and women. That's why in 1998 the Prime Minister Owen Arthur announced that the 28th April would be celebrated as National Heroes Day. The day would serve as a means to recognizing the visionary and pioneering leadership, extraordinary achievement contributions that those people selflessly made Barbadians have made. The 28th April was the date chosen in honour of the birth of Sir Grantley Herbert Adams, one of the ten national heroes remembered every year. The Prime Minister also announced that Trafalgar Square in Bridgetown would be renamed to National Heroes Square.

Sir Grantley Herber Adams

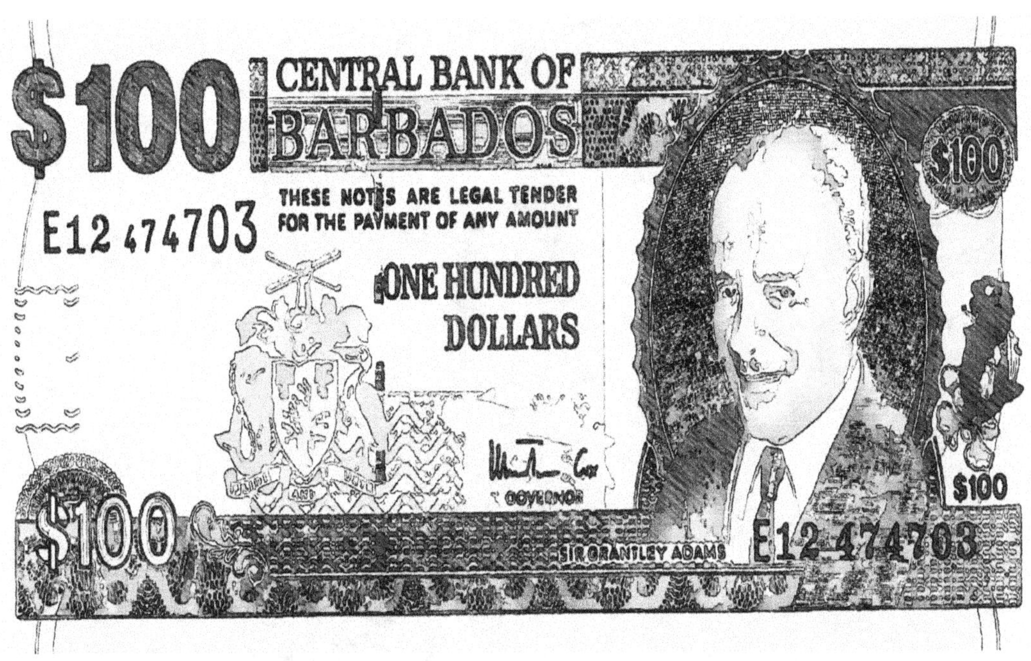

When ministerial government was introduced in 1954, Grantley Herbert Adams was elected first Premier of Barbados. He was one of the most charismatic and outstanding political leaders of the Caribbean Region. Also known as Sir Grantley, who had the ability to understand and relate to the needs of the people in his country. This brilliant and articulate Caribbean leader was not deterred by resistance, he battled relentlessly on behalf of his people and fought against the exploitative and oppressive colonial establishment to guarantee political liberation and economic advancement. With his exceptional debating ability, he penetrated and persuaded the existing colonial power to preserve the rights of Barbadians. In 1970 Mr. Adams was forced to resign from Parliament because of health problems and died in 1976 aged 73. The Queen of England knighted Grantley Adams in 1957 in recognition of his contributions to Barbados and the Caribbean. In honour of the former Premier, Barbados' only airport was named the Grantley Adams International Airport (GAIA) and a statue in front of the Government Headquarters in St. Michael. His image is on the Barbados' $100 bill.

Bussa

Bussa's rebellion was the largest slave revolt in Barbadian history and was the first in 124 years. Little is known about Bussa, if he was married or his exact age. What is known is he was born in Africa in the 18th century, a free man, captured, sold to the British and transported to Barbados as a slave.

He worked as a Ranger at Bayley's Plantation. This gave Bussa more freedom to move around than the average slave, which made it easier for him to plan the rebellion. He was brave, strong and determined for a change. 14th April 1816 Easter Sunday, he led a rebellion with over 400 enslaved people against the British sugar cane Planters. The uprising was carefully planned and was executed by enslaved people at plantations all around Barbados. Bussa was killed in battle, defeated by superior weapons of the colonial army. This slave rebellion was the most significant revolt in the history of Barbados. Bussa became a symbol of the right to live in freedom.

Barbados' National Heroes' Day Traditions and Customs

Schools are involved every year with special historical presentations, spreading awareness of Barbados' national heroes to the youth. Sports like hockey and soccer are typical on this day.

Many celebrations take place at Heroes Square. Food, music and fireworks with many stalls giving others opportunity to discover more about Barbados' culture and the people that have shaped it over the years.

LONDONN

Milann

PARISS

PARISS

Angelees

LONDONN

www.ingramcontent.com/pod-product-compliance
Lightning Source LLC
Chambersburg PA
CBHW080047260726
48658CB00007B/2788